DIANA
PRINCESS OF WALES

Brian Hoey

PITKIN

AN EARL'S DAUGHTER
ROYAL CONNECTIONS

THE PRINCESS OF WALES was not royal by birth, although her family descends from Henry VII. She was born the Honourable Diana Frances Spencer on 1 July 1961 at Park House on the Sandringham Estate in Norfolk. Her parents were the then Viscount Althorp, who was Equerry to The Queen, and the former Honourable Frances Ruth Burke Roche, whose mother had been one of The Queen Mother's ladies-in-waiting.

Diana had two older sisters, Sarah and Jane, and a younger brother, Charles; there was also a brother called John, born in 1960, who survived only ten hours.

Life at Park House was orderly, traditional and aristocratic. The Spencer children lived in the nursery wing on the first floor, set away from the main building, and saw their parents only for an hour in the morning and at tea time, though Diana's mother would occasionally be seen pushing the infant in her pram through the parkland surrounding the house. Childhood playmates included the young princes, Andrew and Edward, who came to swim in the heated pool at Park House. When Diana was just six years old her parents separated and later divorced, the children remaining with their father.

Their life changed dramatically in 1975 when Viscount Althorp succeeded his father as 8th Earl Spencer, Diana becoming Lady Diana, and they moved to the stately home at Althorp in Northamptonshire. The following year Earl Spencer married Raine, Countess of Dartmouth, whose mother was the romantic novelist, Barbara Cartland. Diana went to a finishing school in Switzerland, where she studied domestic science, typing and correspondence, and found plenty of time to enjoy skiing.

below: *The Spencer family coat of arms.*

above: *The wedding of Diana's father, Viscount Althorp, and mother, the Honourable Frances Roche, on 1 June 1954. Diana was deeply affected when, at the age of six, her parents' marriage ended in bitter divorce.*

above: *Diana, aged 13, with her Shetland pony, Soufflé, during a visit to her mother's home in Scotland. A bad fall, in which she broke her arm, put her off riding for many years. However, in later life she always encouraged her sons to ride.*

left: *Diana, aged 8, with her younger brother Charles. Following their parents' separation, Diana had comforted and cared for her brother, and the two of them had become very close.*

right: *Althorp House, in Northamptonshire, became Diana's home in 1975, when her grandfather died and her father inherited the title Earl Spencer. The ancestral home is set in 600 acres.*

LADY DIANA SPENCER
GIRL ABOUT TOWN

WHEN DIANA RETURNED TO BRITAIN from Switzerland she lived in London, sharing an apartment with old school friends. She moved naturally in the society that was described by some as 'Sloane Rangers', so called because much of their leisure time was spent in the fashionable shops and restaurants around Sloane Square. Diana became a nanny to a number of children, and took a three-month cookery course, before joining the Young England Kindergarten as a helper. She enjoyed the social whirl, attending parties in the evenings and going to the country every weekend. Diana would stay with friends, or occasionally go back to Althorp where she would visit her sister Jane, and her husband Sir Robert Fellows, at their house on the estate.

Most of Diana's circle of friends came from similar backgrounds, and when her relationship with The Prince of Wales began they automatically provided her with a shield of protection. Once the media suspected Lady Diana and Prince Charles' new romance, press reporters and cameramen pursued her relentlessly. They besieged her flat at Coleherne Court and followed her everywhere. It was a very testing time for the young Diana.

Diana learned to keep her head down, literally, becoming known as 'Shy Di'. So began the highly intensive media attention which was to continue throughout her life. But once the engagement was official, Diana moved into an apartment in Clarence House, home of the late Queen Mother, where she would be under the protection of the Royal Press Office.

right: *At Ascot 1981, the engaged Lady Diana had already tailored her appearance for the cameras, though she found it difficult to adjust to the intense media attention.*

left: *Lady Diana Spencer and Prince Charles on the steps of Buckingham Palace, after the announcement of their engagement, 24 February 1981. Diana displays her magnificent sapphire and diamond engagement ring.*

right: *Her Majesty The Queen poses for a photograph with Charles and Diana after giving her formal consent to their marriage at a meeting of the Privy Council.*

above: *The Royal Wedding, 29 July 1981. The newly married couple leave St Paul's Cathedral in the 1902 State Landau, accompanied by the pealing of bells, and cheers of happiness from the crowd.*

left: *The Prince and Princess of Wales outside St Paul's. As they stepped out into the summer sunshine the crowd gave a roar of delight which could be heard all over London.*

right: *Urged on by the crowd, Prince Charles kisses Princess Diana's hand on the balcony of Buckingham Palace.*

THE WEDDING of The Prince of Wales and Lady Diana Spencer took place at St Paul's Cathedral on 29 July 1981, barely a month after the bride's 20th birthday. It was a day of joy for everyone: the bride and groom, their families and the millions of people watching on television all over the world. The occasion was a combination of pageantry, high emotion, formal ceremony and vociferous enthusiasm.

Diana was everyone's idea of a fairy-tale bride; her dress, designed by David and Elizabeth Emanuel, was a triumph of ivory silk taffeta, hand embroidered with thousands of tiny mother-of-pearl sequins and pearls, and with a 25-foot train trimmed with sparkling old lace. Diana wore the Spencer family tiara, and diamond earrings borrowed from her mother.

She left Clarence House in the Glass Coach accompanied by her father, to the thunderous cheers of the crowds lining The Mall. At St Paul's the groom was waiting, dressed in the uniform of a Royal Navy commander, with a splendid blue sash of the Order of the Garter. Seated behind him were the 2,650 guests who had been invited to the wedding, including nearly all the crowned heads of Europe.

After the ceremony the couple returned to Buckingham Palace in the 1902 State Landau, while vast crowds pressed against the railings to catch a glimpse of the new Princess of Wales.

They left the Palace in a balloon-bedecked carriage, starting their honeymoon at Broadlands, the Hampshire home of the late Lord Mountbatten, then flying to Gibraltar to join the Royal Yacht *Britannia* for a Mediterranean cruise, and finally joining the Royal Family at Balmoral.

below: *August 1981, the Royal Yacht,* Britannia, *leaves Gibraltar at the beginning of the couple's honeymoon cruise around the Greek Islands.*

FROM THE MOMENT THEY WERE MARRIED, The Prince and Princess of Wales became the focus of public attention to an extent never before experienced in Britain, even by the Royal Family. They became the most closely watched couple in the world, and while Prince Charles was used to being in the spotlight, for Diana it was a new experience. She coped impressively, and soon became the most photographed woman in the world.

Her early days as Princess of Wales were not always easy. She was coming to grips with being a working member of the Royal Family, finding ways to impress her own style upon her new homes at Kensington Palace and Highgrove, and also getting used to the idea that she was now public property, with very little private life.

For one so young, Diana displayed an extraordinary sense of duty, yet she insisted that her prime role in life was to be a good mother to her children. When she and Prince Charles visited Australia in 1983 she refused to leave Prince William behind, saying she was not going to be separated from her baby for such a long period and miss what she regarded as one of the most important parts of his life. It showed that The Princess had a mind of her own and was not prepared to be merely a pretty accessory.

left: *This portrait of Charles and Diana was photographed by Snowdon at Highgrove, in Gloucestershire, which was the couple's first home. Charles wears the uniform of a Royal Navy commander, with a blue sash of the Order of the Garter.*

right: *In Australia, October 1985. To the great delight of everyone present, Charles whirls Diana around the floor as they dance to Stevie Wonder's 'Isn't She Lovely'. Diana wears Queen Mary's emerald and diamond choker as a headband, having discovered that her tiara had been left at home.*

above: *The Princess of Wales, in Canberra, Australia, greets the excited crowd during her first overseas royal tour, in 1983. She was amazed by the attention she received during this visit.*

A DEVOTED MOTHER

'MY BELOVED PRINCES'

left: *The proud Princess of Wales holds Prince William in her sitting room at Kensington Palace, February 1983. She knew that the role of raising William to be a monarch in the new millennium was going to be the most important of her life.*

far left: *A family portrait, taken in the garden at Highgrove.*

below: *The Princess of Wales with Prince Harry during a holiday in Majorca, 1987. The closeness of the relationship between Diana and her sons was always apparent.*

DIANA'S NATURAL ROLE IN LIFE was motherhood. She had always had a special affinity with children of all ages and she never doubted for a moment that she was intended to be a mother. Speaking about her children she once said, 'They mean everything to me' and later added, 'I always feed my children love and affection – it's so important'.

Although the royal marriage ended in divorce there were many times when the couple enjoyed great happiness together. One such time was at 9.03 p.m. on 21 June 1982, when Diana gave birth to her first son, Prince William, in the private Lindo Wing of St Mary's Hospital in London. Prince Charles broke with royal tradition by being present at the birth, and it was also the first time that an heir-presumptive had been born in hospital. Both Diana and Prince Charles were overjoyed.

They were affectionate parents and Diana said she had found her true destiny. She was never happier than when she was playing with William, whom she called Wills. Two years later, on 15 September 1984, Harry was born.

above: *Diana with Harry on their visit to Thorpe Park, 13 April 1993. She loved to have fun with her boys, and wanted to bring them up to know a 'normal' life despite their extraordinary destiny.*

right: *During their visit to Canada in October 1991, Diana, William and Harry visit Niagara Falls and take a ride on board the* Maid of The Mist.

Off duty, Diana would attempt to shrug off the rigid controls of royal protocol and relax with her sons. She was determined that, although they would never forget who they were, they should have as normal an upbringing as possible. She took them to the cinema, letting them choose the films they wanted to see, and introduced them to the delights of fast food hamburger cafés, where she queued with other parents to serve herself. She was a thoroughly modern mother who refused to allow her royal role to interfere with the ordinary, everyday joys of bringing up her children.

Diana turned up at the princes' annual sports day, kicked off her shoes and ran barefoot in the mothers' race – which she won, to her sons' great delight. When the time came for Prince William to go away to school, Diana expressed a very clear preference for Eton. It was near enough to London that she could see him frequently, while allowing him to become an ordinary boarder. Both she and Prince Charles insisted that he should be treated the same way as the other pupils.

Diana impressed upon her sons their connection with the principality whose name they shared, telling them never to forget what they were: Prince William and Prince Harry of Wales. She took William on his first official visit to Wales – on St David's Day 1991 – and later took both boys to Cardiff to watch the Welsh rugby team in action.

She instilled in her sons her own sense of public awareness from an early age, and showed them, at first hand, how the underprivileged are forced to live by taking them with her to a Seamen's Mission centre for the homeless. It was a salutary experience for the young princes, but one which she felt was necessary in their ongoing training for their future lives.

Diana will be remembered in many different ways, but undoubtedly the most important legacy of her extraordinary life is her two sons, William and Harry.

right: *Prince Harry and Prince William on holiday in Balmoral, August 1997. It was during this holiday that they heard of their mother's tragic death.*

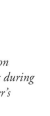

AS SHE FREELY ADMITTED, Diana was not an intellectual. But despite her lack of academic achievement she possessed a quick wit and an understanding that enabled her to survive those early years and adapt to her new role, while her empathy with the public prevented her from being dismissed as merely a 'walking clothes-horse'.

Diana believed that the monarchy should be in touch with the people, and she won many hearts with her spontaneity and genuine warmth. She was a tactile person who loved to give a hug or a kiss, whether to a child in a Nigerian village or an old lady in a British geriatric ward. People from all walks of life and of all ages identified with her, for her sense of style as well as for the compassion she showed to the sick and the suffering, and to those who had been the outcasts of society.

The public turned out in droves whenever and wherever she appeared, and she always found time to stop and talk, often delaying her official programme in order to chat with people who had waited hours to see her.

It was her common touch, combined with her grace and aristocracy, that made her so popular with the press. They adored her, and followed her wherever she went, knowing that she would always provide them with a winning picture or story. She never let them down. Some of them whom she grew to trust, and took into her confidence, became personal friends who would mourn her in death as much as they had revered her in life.

left: *People thronged to see Diana whenever she appeared in public, and she always reciprocated by being friendly and approachable.*

right: *During her visit to Canada in 1991, Diana greets an elderly woman. The Princess showed particular concern for the old and the frail, and communicated with them openly and directly.*

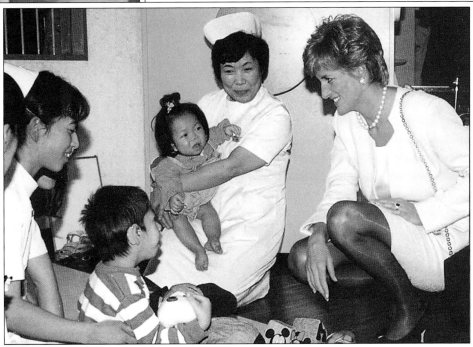

left: *Tour to Japan, 1995. Diana always made a point of visiting schools and hospitals when touring foreign countries, and the children always responded to her warmth and compassion.*

IF EVER A PERSON could justifiably claim to be a one-woman fashion industry, that person must have been Diana, Princess of Wales. Almost single-handedly she rejuvenated the British fashion scene, practically from the moment she first stepped onto the royal stage.

Legions of women, from Japan to Jersey, faithfully copied her style down to the tiniest detail. When she appeared in a 'Robin Hood' type of hat in the early 80s, identical copies were bought in their thousands, and when she, mischievously, wore a diamond necklace as a headband, jewellers throughout the world were inundated the next day with enquiries for replicas.

Diana never saw herself as a fashion icon and she disliked the description, believing it detracted from her more serious side. She said she never followed fashion, only dressing 'for the job in hand'. It is true that she was not a follower but a trend-setter, and if she was set up as an icon it was only because women so admired her innate sense of style and her ability to choose what was right for her. She managed to combine a modern look with the requirements of royal dignity and cool elegance. The demands of her position necessitated a large wardrobe, and Diana was determined to show the very best of British design and manufacture wherever she went on her overseas tours, performing an extraordinary service for the fashion industry and bringing a new glamorous image to the Royal Family.

She was not dressed exclusively by British designers. Diana was often seen, in recent years, in outfits by Christian Dior, John Galliano, Gianni Versace and Jacques Azagury, as well as those she wore from Bruce Oldfield and Catherine Walker.

Diana was fascinated by showbusiness and the arts and missed no opportunity to mix with stars of stage and screen. Ballet was her first love, and as Patron of the English National Ballet she played an active role in the organization, often turning up to watch rehearsals and staying behind to talk with the dancers. She once wistfully remarked that she would have loved to have been a ballet dancer but 'at 5ft 10ins I'm too tall'. So when she sprang a surprise Christmas present for Prince Charles in 1985 by dancing on stage with Wayne Sleep, she was also achieving a life-time ambition. Some years later at a reception at the White House in Washington she partnered John Travolta on the dance floor and afterwards both said it was a 'dream come true'.

left: *Wearing a cocktail dress by Christina Stambolian, Diana arrives for a dinner at the Serpentine Gallery, June 1994.*

right: *The Princess of Wales attends the premiere of the film 'Hot Shots' in November 1991.*

below: *The Princess's beauty, elegance and style are much in evidence when she arrives at a gala dinner, in Chicago, wearing a purple Versace dress.*

It was Diana's first change in hairstyle that seemed to transform her the most. Just after the birth of Prince Harry her pageboy hair-cut was replaced by a new style that was classic, sophisticated and totally stunning. The Diana look had arrived; the photographic image had been created.

In June 1997, responding to a suggestion by Prince William, Diana assigned Christie's to auction 79 of her dresses, raising $3.25 million (£1,960,150) for charity. They ranged from short cocktail dresses to formal ball-gowns and included her favourite: a Victor Edelstein creation in duchesse satin with matching bolero jacket, which sold for $90,500 (£54,436).

below: *The Princess attends a gala evening in aid of Cancer Research at Bridgewater House, London, in November 1995. She wears a dress by Jacques Azagury, a French designer based in Knightsbridge.*

above: *Wearing a pink Versace suit, Diana arrives at the Angel Roffo Cancer Hospital in Buenos Aires, Argentina, November 1995. Her neat, tailored working suits showed a business-like approach to her busy schedule.*

right: *Diana, Princess of Wales arrives at the Elyseé Palace, in Paris, 1988. She is wearing an appliquéd dress and matching bolero by Victor Edelstein.*

A MODERN PRINCESS
DIANA'S NEW LIFE

WITH THE COLLAPSE OF HER MARRIAGE in 1992 – separation, followed in 1996 by divorce – Diana set out to find a new life for herself as a single parent. She wanted to create an independent role outside the Royal Family but, as the mother of a future King, she was never completely able to shed her responsibilities, or her image throughout the world as 'Princess Di'.

She formed a number of unfortunate relationships which were quickly terminated and she realized that unqualified love and loyalty would come only from her sons. Diana worked hard at keeping physically fit by visiting a gymnasium most days, and she sought the company of people whom she believed would not try to exploit her.

She made many visits to the United States where her popularity never waned, and where she continued to be treated as royalty. Americans saw her as both an innocent victim and a winner in the divorce battle, and acclaimed her as a great survivor and a successful single mother.

Once the publicity of the marriage break-up had died down Diana began working towards her goal, which was to be taken seriously in her own right. She had discussions with political leaders, such as President Nelson Mandela of South Africa, and finally she achieved her aim, taking a role on the international stage as an unofficial but highly influential ambassadress.

Her crusade for the world-wide banning of landmines touched the public conscience in a way that nothing else had done. She had picked on exactly the right subject at precisely the right moment.

above: *In May 1992, during a solo visit to Egypt, The Princess is photographed alone in the desert in front of the Giza pyramids.*

right: *February 1992, during the visit by The Prince and Princess of Wales to India. Diana, aware that her marriage is coming to an end, is pictured alone at the Taj Mahal, the huge mausoleum known as the world's greatest monument to love.*

right: *Diana greets the famous rock singer Phil Collins at her 30th birthday celebrations on 1 July 1991.*

AT ONE TIME The Princess of Wales was involved with over a hundred charities, which she liked to call her 'Family of Organizations'.

At the height of her working life, her patronages included such disparate bodies as Barnardos, Birthright, the British Deaf Association (for whom she learnt sign language), the Leprosy Mission, the Malcolm Sargent Cancer Fund for Children, The Princess of Wales Children's Health Camp in Rotorua (New Zealand), Turning Point, Help the Aged, Centrepoint, AIDS Crisis Trust and the Great Ormond Street Hospital for Sick Children.

When she accepted an invitation to become patron of a charity, she became a tireless worker and a fearless fighter on its behalf.

Turning Point was perhaps one of the most unlikely groups for a member of the Royal Family to support. It was the largest national voluntary organization providing help for men and women with drug and alcohol-related problems, and for people recovering from mental illness. When Diana was asked to join them she agreed without hesitation, on the condition that she was not to be merely another royal figurehead, but an active participant in all their work. She raised the profile of Turning Point dramatically and as their Chief Executive, Les Rudd, explained, 'We have an unpopular client group and without The Princess's personal involvement we would never have attracted the public's sympathy to such an extent'.

above: During a briefing at the American Red Cross Headquarters, Washington DC, in June 1997, Diana gives a speech on landmines and the impressions she had gained when visiting Angola. This was followed by a dinner at which $650,000 (£399,000) was raised for the landmines campaign.

left: *The Princess of Wales at the paediatric intensive care unit at St Mary's Hospital, London, raising funds for Cosmic. Her service to her charities was always wholehearted.*

right: *At a hostel for abandoned children in São Paolo, Diana holds an HIV positive child, an action aimed at breaking down the taboos surrounding AIDS. She felt she had a destiny to help the suffering, and was aware of her power to move people's hearts.*

Diana chose to become actively involved with Centrepoint, a charity which concentrates on providing accommodation for homeless young people who are considered to be at risk. She said 'Nothing gives me greater pleasure than to try to help the most vulnerable people in society'.

In 1993 Diana announced her retirement from public life and relinquished her position with nearly all her charities. She retained a handful which she continued to support and work for until the day she died.

One of the most courageous and important of Diana's public appearances was undoubtedly when she decided to open the first specialist AIDS ward in Britain. AIDS was, at that time, the unmentionable disease and few people were prepared to be associated with its care and treatment. The Princess sent shock waves throughout the world when she shook hands with patients suffering from AIDS – and did so without wearing gloves. By that single action she demonstrated that people had no need to fear that the disease might be transmitted simply by touch. From that moment her commitment to the cause was total; she helped raise millions of pounds and, more importantly, she increased the public's awareness and understanding at a time when fear and prejudice were commonplace.

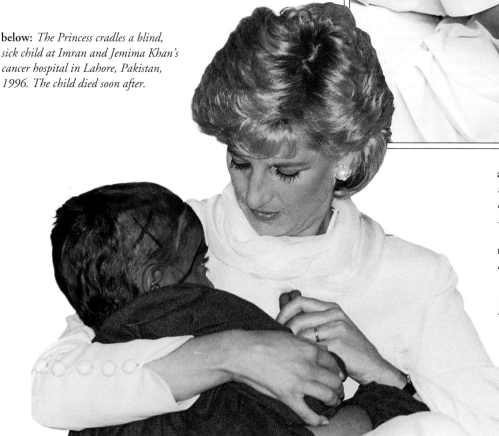

below: *The Princess cradles a blind, sick child at Imran and Jemima Khan's cancer hospital in Lahore, Pakistan, 1996. The child died soon after.*

above: *The Princess delights in the attention of school children at a Hindu temple in Neasden, London, June 1997.*

right: *The Princess receives a kiss from a member of the 'untouchable' caste in India, 1992. She was a touchstone of hope for victims of poverty and injustice.*

When Diana visited a leprosy hospital in Jakarta, Indonesia and another in Nigeria, and comforted those suffering from this most disfiguring of diseases, she never once flinched or drew away from close contact. She said, 'I am trying to show in a simple action that they are not reviled, nor we repulsed'.

It is difficult to overestimate the impact that Diana made on the causes she espoused. As a fundraiser she was unequalled; her presence at a function ensured that all the tickets would be sold in hours.

She worked indefatigably for the Royal Marsden Hospital Cancer Fund and insisted that part of the proceeds of the auction of her

dresses in New York should go to the hospital. The rest of the money went to another of her favourite charities, AIDS Crisis Trust.

Diana's concern for the dispossessed and the under-privileged knew no national boundaries. Together with her friends Imran and Jemima Khan she visited Pakistan to support their efforts in famine relief; and after meeting Mother Teresa in New York, she travelled to India to see for herself the living conditions of some of the poorest people in the world.

But it was when she visited Angola and Bosnia that people realised how sound her instinct was. She had begun her campaign for the

right: *In June 1997, Diana joins Mother Teresa for a walk-about in the Bronx, New York. Diana's charitable works were highly praised by Mother Teresa, and parallels were often drawn between them by the media. It was poignant that these two women who cared about the same things died within the same week.*

banning of landmines without any official backing, but soon governments around the world were responding to her call.

In Bosnia she met and comforted mutilated victims and bereaved widows and orphans with a sensitive professionalism that showed clearly how much she understood the anguish all around her. It was to be her last crusade.

When she was accused of interfering in political issues, Diana replied, 'I am a humanitarian, I lead from the heart'.

left: *Diana never shied away from deprivation and pain, and involved herself actively in her charity work. Here she visits the Red Cross Nemazuva Child Feeding Centre in Zimbabwe, July 1993.*

below: *Wearing protective body armour and visor, The Princess visits a minefield, in Angola, that is being cleared by the Halo Trust, January 1997. Her campaign to ban landmines generated international approval, and prompted a number of governments into action.*

above: *On 6 September 1997, the coffin containing the body of Diana, Princess of Wales is carried on a gun-carriage to Westminster Abbey. Adorning the coffin are wreaths from Prince William and Prince Harry, and from Diana's brother, Earl Spencer.*

right: *Her Majesty The Queen outside Westminster Abbey with the Dean of Westminster, the Very Rev Dr Wesley Carr, who led the funeral service.*

DIANA DIED IN A CAR CRASH with Dodi Fayed on 31 August 1997, in Paris. Few events in Britain's history have produced the sense of national dismay and bewilderment that followed. People travelled from all parts of the country to pay tribute to The Princess. Thousands of bouquets of flowers were placed at the gates of Buckingham Palace and Kensington Palace, and people queued for up to twelve hours to sign the books of condolence at St James's Palace.

The Queen appeared on television and spoke movingly of her former daughter-in-law. 'She was an exceptional and gifted human being. In good times and bad, she never lost her capacity to smile and laugh, nor to inspire others with her warmth and kindness.'

The funeral, described by Buckingham Palace as 'a unique service for a unique person', was an inspiring combination of traditional ritual and informality.

The coffin containing Diana's body was carried on a First World War gun-carriage drawn by six black horses and nine members of The King's Troop Royal Horse Artillery, and flanked by a bearer party of Welsh Guardsmen. Thousands, many of whom had camped out overnight in order to get a good position, watched silently, and threw flowers into their path. As the cortège passed through Wellington Arch and down Constitution Hill, The Queen and three generations of the Royal Family emerged from Buckingham Palace.

The Prince of Wales, Prince Philip, Prince William and Prince Harry, together with Diana's brother, Earl Spencer, joined the cortège and walked behind the coffin to Westminster Abbey. They were followed by a throng of representatives of many of her charities.

The service was simple and dignified, with Diana's favourite hymns and poems read by her sisters. Diana's brother gave a penetrating and passionate address. The 2,000-strong congregation included politicians, showbusiness celebrities, personal friends and representatives from her charities.

For many the most poignant element of the ceremony was the Princes' wreath on the coffin: a small ring of white roses bearing the word 'Mummy'.

As the choir sang a haunting anthem the coffin was carried away. At the door the procession stopped and an absolute silence descended – a silence that was respected by millions throughout the world.

Diana's body was laid to rest at Althorp, on a peaceful and secluded island in the middle of a lake.

left: *The Prince of Wales, Prince Harry, Earl Spencer, Prince William and The Duke of Edinburgh follow as the coffin is carried into the Abbey.*

below: *What began as a few bouquets outside Kensington Palace grew into a vast sea of flowers, as mourners came in their thousands to pay their final respects to Diana.*

THE PEOPLE'S PRINCESS
A TRIBUTE

THE DEATH OF DIANA, Princess of Wales unleashed an expression of public feeling on an unprecedented scale. Nothing had prepared the people for the shock of losing such a vital, beautiful young woman who had everything to live for. People of all ages had been able to identify with this member of the Royal Family, as a glamorous leader of fashion, a dedicated mother and more recently as the undisputed champion of the under-privileged, the handicapped and the elderly. She did more than had ever been done before to focus attention on what were previously unmentionable subjects, and the practical and constructive way in which she displayed her compassion and sympathy was a fine demonstration of modern royalty at work.

Diana had star quality, of that there was no doubt. She became the most pursued woman in the world and gave the impression of enjoying her celebrity status, even though she claimed not to understand why so many people felt so affectionate towards her. Perhaps it was this very innocence that made her so attractive. She occasionally gave the outward appearance of being tough, and she herself said she would 'fight like a tiger' for what she believed in. But another of the qualities that emerged was her vulnerability, and it was this that made so many people spring to her defence. She never lacked friends to take her part and champion her cause, and there was never a shortage of volunteers anxious to protect and cherish her. Much of her international appeal came about because those who came into contact with her felt a natural instinct to look after her, even when she protested that she did not need protecting.

Diana was always a woman who acted from the heart, and the world loved her for it. She possessed a natural aura of accessibility, and was never afraid to show her emotions. Ordinary men and women felt they could approach her without any fear of rebuttal; she positively encouraged people to talk to her and touch her.

Diana has been described as one of the nation's greatest assets and her appearance was one of her most important attributes. Even when her behaviour was unpredictable, she was forgiven because of her beauty and style.

Her most important role was raising her small family. Everything else was secondary to the welfare of her sons and no one was ever left in any doubt as to her priorities. William and Harry came first and in spite of the pressures she lived under – and they would have increased as the boys grew older – that would not have changed. She knew that William's position as a future king was unique and that he was going to need all the encouragement and help she could give him. She was prepared to subjugate her own ambitions to his happiness and security.

If Diana seemed to rebel against a protocol and tradition that appeared to be stuffy and restrictive, it struck a chord with young people, who felt she was striking a blow for them as well as for herself. And when she comforted the sick, the maimed and the abused, those around her knew that this was not an act, neither was she merely going through the routine of a well-rehearsed and programmed public appearance. Although her duties were necessarily choreographed down to the last detail, her concern was obviously genuine and she managed to communicate her true feelings.

How will she be remembered and what were her most significant achievements? It would be invidious to single out from her many good works just one and name it as the most important. On the international scene, if there is a successful conclusion to her landmines campaign, that would be a fitting memorial; or if there is a breakthrough in the treatment of AIDS or cancer. Perhaps her involvement in child care and famine relief will result in greater public awareness.

Diana will be remembered as an inspirational woman who once said she wanted to be known as a 'Queen of Hearts'. Perhaps in death that is exactly what she has become.

left: January 1997, at an orthopaedic workshop in Luanda, Angola, Diana befriends 13-year-old Sandra Tigica, a landmine victim.

Diana photographed for British Vogue *magazine by Patrick Demarchelier.*